Echoes From Another Shore

GENEVA
ENSIGN

ECHOES FROM ANOTHER SHORE
Copyright © 2019 Geneva Ensign

All rights reserved. No part of this publication may be reproduced, stored in a retrieval system or transmitted, in any form or by any means, electronic, mechanical, photocopying, recording, or otherwise, without the written permission of the author, except in the case of a reviewer, who may quote brief passages in a review or study group.

Copies can be ordered from the author:
Geneva Ensign email: gee_b@shaw.ca

Printed in Canada by:
UBR Services Printing & Copies
9618B Bottom Wood Lake Road
Lake Country, British Columbia V4V 1S7
www.ubrservices.ca
2019

AM I A MYTH?

Am I a myth,
A non-existent me
That cries to know
My name,
My identity, my being,
My essence?

Can a non-existent something
Cry
Or
Are these echoes
From
Another
Shore?

Is there a pool of Self,
Unknown,
Unchartered seas
Within?

Waiting For The Word

I sit waiting
For dictation,
Words of Knowing
To softly fall,
One by one
Upon the breeze.

And I will capture them
Upon this page.

The Word that created
All of creation,
is
On-going,
Ever
Creating me
Anew.

DYING AND HEAVEN

When I was young,
I sat in church
And heard men say
They were awaiting
The day they could die
And be in heaven
Walking streets of gold,
Wearing jeweled crowns.
Heaven
And I shuddered.
Heaven,
An escape from life?
Heaven?
And I shuddered,
Thinking that I did not want to die
Before I had lived.

GUARDIANS

I have many guardians
Of my Soul

In silent shadows shrieking
Out their do's and don'ts
Pursuing, guarding,

Hounds of heaven?
Hounds of hell?

Where Is The Me?

Where is the me
That lies hammerlocked,
Struggling
Between twin strangleholds of
My Id
And very Super Ego?

With You, I Need No Defenses

With you,
I need no defenses,
No walls to protect
My Inner Self.

You have heard
My rambling thoughts,
Uncensored,
Listening, patient,
While I sorted and sifted
Myself
For meaning,
For truth.

I have no need to hide
From you
The cobwebs and the dust
Nor do I rush
To straighten or to sweep
The corridors of my
Inner closets
Before you come.

You know
As much as I
About myself,
Almost.

You, being you,
No stranger,
Your truth cannot hurt,
Will not hurt,
Because
With you, I'm not pretending
To be
What I am not.

Your gentle probes
Can be accepted
Or rejected
According to my truth
About myself.

I will know if
What you say
Holds truth

Even if I do not understand
Its truth
At the moment.

To withhold your truth
From me
When I am asking,
Hoping to protect
Me from myself,
Only makes me doubt,
For a time,
The reality of my knowing
And delays,
For a time,
My search
For me.

I Walk In The Cemetery

I walk in the cemetery on the hill
Among the gravestones
That whisper quiet lies.
Some say, "In his service."
Some say, "Beloved by all."
Some say, "Remembered forever."
Lies, lies, lying.

I walk in the cemetery
Among the silent gravestones
That whisper quiet lies.
I walk, I am not lying. I walk,
Yet without fear, a gravestone myself.

The sun is warm; the air caressing,
Fingers soft upon my eyes, my lips.
I walk with death and feel no fear.
I feel nothing, no-thing.
No emotion—no fear, no love, no desire,
Neutral, awaiting—fear or love—
Some sign of life, waiting to be.
Waiting, thinking, while waiting,
That in the tomorrow of tomorrows,
I want no gravestone to whisper
That I have lived.

How many years
Must a gravestone shout
Silently
That I have lived
Before the shout becomes the truth?
How many years?
An eternity
Is not enough.

I walk in the cemetery
Among the silent gravestones
Mere existence
Is not a life,
A spark only,
Not a flame.

I walk in the cemetery
Among the silent gravestones…
Single ones, double ones
Some complete, neat, even.
Mr. and Mrs. lie here
Together
An eternity of togetherness,
An eternity of aloneness.

Some double gravestones
Are only half,
Incomplete inscriptions cry
"Come, lie with me,"
Add your name next to mine."
Waiting,
Wanting
To fulfill in death
A completion
Not attained in life.
Two people,
Corpses, silent and alone
Can lie in a double grave
As in a double bed,
Alone in life
Alone in death
Alone,
Dead.

I walk out of the cemetery on the hill
Where silent gravestones
Still whisper quiet lies.
I walk out of the cemetery
Where silent gravestones wait,
Yet
For me.

I stroll on the hill and discover
Nestled in the lee of the
Old priests' building,
Crumbling and tall,
Sentinel against the night,
Red poppies, bright and beautiful,
Despite the autumn's killing frost.
Blood red, the poppies,
Defying death, they stand, erect,
Affirming in this autumn day
That life and love are yet to be.

I will live and I will love
While yet alive
And death will need no silent gravestones
To whisper quiet lies.

On Growing

Just add water
Nothing more
The sun can do the rest,
Nothing more to
Mix or stir
Create or blend
Shape or cut or mutilate.
Water and sun
Sun and water.
Nothing more
Nothing more.

Labour Pains

I am having labour pains;
I am giving birth to me.
The struggle to "be" is real, overpowering,
Immediate.
It is an inner force, a drive, that will not,
Does not,
Stop.

My body tenses;
An ache across my lower back,
A rigidity to my legs;
My muscles strain against themselves;
My shoulders ache.

There is no pain, and yet there is—
A pain of intensity,
An inward turning, a straining
To know,
To understand,
To be.

At times the pain ceases,
My body relaxes,
Tranquil for the moment, yet
Waiting for another seizure.
My body tenses again.

My body knows how much
It can take; it relaxes,
Before continuing
The process of giving birth
To me.

I cannot stop this force;
I am in its power, a part of its process.
It will continue,
With or without
My cooperation.
Once labour has started,
No one can halt its force;
No one can re-direct
The channel,
The path to being.

There is no other way,
But out,
Through,
Completed
I cannot sidetrack
This birth.
It has me in its
Grip.

Walls Within Walls

I am a fortress
Walls, within walls, within walls
Strong walls, tall walls,
Carefully constructed
To protect
My Inner Self
My treasure, my perfection.

I am a fortress
Walls, within walls, within walls
Strong walls, tall walls.
No alien eyes
Can penetrate
The darkness,
Can evaluate, suggest
Or criticize.

I am a fortress,
Walls, within walls, within walls
Strong walls, tall walls
Protection against change
Protection of perfection.

I am a fortress,
But
Walls, within walls, within walls

Without windows
Create darkness.
No rays of sunlight
Can penetrate
Musty corners
And
No rays of truth
Can dance with dust
Illuminating, purifying.

Has my Inner Self
Been deformed by darkness?
Or is she
Protected perfection?
The prisoner
Is growing restless…

Oh, restless Self,
Grow stronger yet;
Fight hard to crack the walls with truth,
Your only weapon.
Destroy the fortress and the prison
For
Neither protected nor prisoner
Need thou be.

Surprise Attack

I am not a fighter
But
When some intrepid soul
Sends sharp arrows
Into well-defended regions
Of myself,
I stand, hurt
Not quite defenseless.
Then
A waterfall of tears
Cascades from angry eyes
Catching the intruder
By surprise,
Engulfing him.
And
I know it will be long
Before he,
Retreating in soggy disarray,
Remaining arrows scattering,
Will dare to venture near again
My well-protected
Territory.

Mirror Reflection

I am a mirror--that's all.
If you do not want to Know
What I've been reflecting to you about yourself,
Then keep your eyes tightly closed.
And that's all right.

If you are indecisive about Knowing,
Then it may be best to squint.
And that's all right too.

If, however, you do want to Know,
To experience the reality of you,
Then look deeply,
Searchingly,
Eyes wide open.

A mirror gives no gifts;
It only reflects what is.

I Reason Against The Reason

I reason against the
Reason
of my love.

Yet, love
Is beyond reason,
Beyond my logic and
My mind.

It is.

Free Spirits Are Timid Creatures

When I was young,
My free spirit tried its wings
Wheeling a bicycle with giggly abandon
Around a corner
Only to come crashing to the roadway
Blood painting the gravel red.

Hurt and alone,
Crying for help,
I ran to my mother.

"Don't drip blood on my new carpet!"
She cried in alarm,
Crushing my spirit, negating my need.
Memory erased the rest,
Although I am sure she washed the cut
And applied the sterile bandage.

And if, in my hurt
And in my aloneness,
I run to you,
What then?

Spirits, free spirits, are timid creatures;
Frightened by logic and by reason,
Also at times by their own desiring,
They flee
To the safety of hidden nooks
And well-known inner spaces,
Careful not to venture forth
Too soon again.

And if, in my hurt
And in my aloneness,
I run to you,
What then?

Hurt, Tears, Anger

Hurt covers anger;
Tears cover hurt.
I've been crying for years.
I've been hurting for years.
I've been angry for years.

I become angry
When you don't accept me,
Not what I do, or say,
But me.
I have not always known
The difference
Between me and what I say or do
But now I am beginning to
And I believe
You don't accept the essence of me.

My tears embarrass, frustrate you;
My emotions do the same,
Unless they are focused in you
And only then
If they are accepting of you,
Enhancing, Flattering,
Ego-building.

Do I accept you?
That's hard to say.
I think I do.
I like your eyes, your emotions,
However guarded,
Your times when, in spite of yourself,
You seem to feel deeply
Or
Act spontaneously.

But the shell of you,
I reject;
Your irritability,
Your judgmentalness,
Your need for order, perfection
Yet you can't accomplish it in your
Environment or in yourself,
Your fidgetiness,
Constant movement and talking,

Planning, controlling,
Your negativism.
You see more wrong than right,
A crooked seam, a jagged edge,
All these
Set me in motion
And then I reject
Seemingly you,
But not the essence of you.

What you can be
What you are at times
Is what I want.
I reject
The you that
Rejects me,
The you that
Will not listen
To the cry in me,
But only to my words.

You say I must be rational,
Logical,
And when I'm not,
You say
I'm only feeling—and that
You reject,
Again.

I want, oh I want
To love you.
You keep me away,
Far away.
Let me be me!

Who Knows?

The owl,
All eyes;
Eyes that penetrate
The darkness.

The owl,
Symbol of wisdom,
Looking,
Seeing,
Knowing.

Oh, owl,
Is looking
Seeing?
Is seeing
Knowing?

The owl,
Eyes,
All eyes.
Do they penetrate
The darkness?

Whoooooooooooo
Can?

I Know More About You Now

I know more about
You now,
Your warmth and caring
Seemingly inexhaustible,
Ended only by
What?

That limit is not
Mine to say
And if we know,
And push beyond
A pre-fixed limit,
We will have reached
Another place,
A space
Beyond the present.

EGO MONSTER

You don't see
me;
You don't even see
Yourself.

You are blind,
But stand
Affixed
In the center
Of your world
Reaching out
Engulfing,
Devouring,
Distorting,
Twisting
All,
Everything,
To satisfy
Your insatiable appetite.

Massive,
Ego monster,
You.

OPT OUT

When the reality of life
Becomes a
Stranger
To the longings of your soul,

Opt out.

Stop your world;
Wrap your cocoon
Of dreams
Warmly around you.

Rest
Renew
Recreate
Your
Self.

My Self Is Heavy

I do not want you
Nor your problems
On my shoulders;
I can hardly carry
My Self.

My Self is heavy,
Burdened with the chore
Of living,
Heavy, hurting.

The vapor that was
Yesterday
Is gone,
Evaporated.
It must be somewhere,
That energy,
That longing
To be,
Just to be.

It's hard to believe
That joy can turn
To sorrow;
Did joy escape
To someone else
When sorrow came my way?

Is sorrow always
Lurking
In the background,
Waiting
For an opening, a chance
To overpower
In moments least expected?

Why can't I be
Equally surprised
By joy?

Words Are Barriers

Words
Are
Barriers
Between you and me,
Keeping us from
Experiencing the
Reality
Of
Each other.

Words are words are words,
Endless,
Meaningless,
Intellectual games
Until
Words become experienced
And
Experience becomes
Connective tissue
Binding
Us
Together.

Duty Walks With Heavy Tread

Duty walks with heavy tread
Upon the path of life;
He brings a frown upon his brow
And fills the air with strife.

He cannot dance with airy feet
Nor can he laugh with head thrown back,
But speaks of self and shoulds.
And writes with poison pen
Upon this restless heart of mine.

I do not want unending words,
Life's graffiti,
Imprinted on my soul.
Can duty ever change his tread,
Cast off his frown
And dance
For life, for joy, for love?

Dance Of The Rings

With this ring, I thee wed.
Small circles of gold slipped on fingers
Lovingly,
Expectantly,
Naively.
Small circles of gold,
Symbol of completion, wholeness
Everlasting love.

Two circles
Interlocked, moving
In tangential autonomy
Or
Locked in
Unending struggle
For completeness.

Pilgrim At Tinker Creek

Pilgrim at Tinker Creek,
I too,
Have trekked
The muddy paths
Along the river of light,
Haltingly stumbling
Through the misty shadows
Eyes straining
To pierce
The darkness.

Slipping grasping
But there's no/thing (except myself?)
Falling
Rising again,
Faint, but drawn
Moth-like
Toward the light.

Ever
Forward,
If forward it be,
Glimpsing occasional
Splinters
Of quick-silvery truth—

Unfolding awareness—
But
Its faint flickers
Elude
My searching eyes,
Hide-and-seekingly
Teasing.

Elusive dreams?
Ultimate truths?
Illusions?
Pilgrim at Tinker Creek,
Must I travel alone
Along your well-worn, but
Unchartered, pathways?

Cannot you my teacher be?
My guide? At least,
A signpost drive,
Warning me in foggy lands of bogs
Or turns
Or pitfalls
Along the way!
* * *

New pilgrim,
You,
Alone
Must travel.
You cannot read the signposts
You so urgently request
Until you learn
The elusive language
Of experience.

And
When you Know,
By experience,
That age-old language
Its words will only confirm
That which you have learned already.

They cannot warn you
Of that
You know not of
Nor
Can they instruct
Nor foretell
The future.
They only
Confirm
The past.
But

When you Know
And
When I Know
By experience
We can share that which has been.

And if
In one shining moment
We stand together
In a ray of truth
Experiencing
What is,
Words cast aside, unneeded
That is ecstasy.

ODE TO A LISTENER

Earlier, at Pilgrim Creek,
I said that when I fell,
There was
No/thing, no/body, except myself
To cling to.
Not quite true
For there was you.
You were,
Just were.
You listened,
You dried the falling tears.
You held me.
You gently probed at times.
No more.
It was enough.
You were.
And so I am.

Desire Is A Vapor

Desire is a vapor
Intangible and strong,
Energizing force
Arising from
The very core of
Me.

Indomitable,
Total longing,
Beyond the call of duty,
That sentinel of mind.

Misty particles
That dance
And touch
And separate,
Engulfing me.

LOCKED BOX

Catch, if you can,
The vapor called desire
Lock it in a box
And throw away the key.

Metal box—
Freezing
Tears
Icy drops.

Metal box
Heat
Powerful explosion
Force of energy
Release.

WHO ARE YOU?

Who are you
Who holds me fast,
Oh, unseen person,
Black,
Dark hand
That fetters mine?

Dark upon dark
In a corner you hide
Unseen
Unknown
Constraining me

Oh sun,
Allow your
Penetrating rays
To illumine
This dark corner
So I can
See!

LET ME GO!

Let me go,
Release me
From my inhibitions!

Release your Self,
The shadow answered.
You, alone,
Can unlock the door,
Unfasten the chains
That you have so carefully
Secured around your Self,
Immobilizing
Your thoughts
Your emotions,
Your raging feelings.

Free your Self
To think
To feel
To know and
To explore.

Release your Self,
Let go.

DO I HAVE TIME TO WAIT?

Do I have time to wait?
Time an eternity yet a moment
Now.
Life is now.

I breathe,
I cry,
I yearn
Now.
For what?
Vague, uneasy
Longings.

Am I brave enough to know my longings?
Identify my desires?
Change my yearnings into dreams;
My dreams into reality?
It's safer to yearn,
Feeling, unwilling to act.

I am marking time,
Waiting for
Each day to pass;
Maybe tomorrow will
Bring something,
Someone
To free me
From my bondage
Of yearning;
Someone to propel me
To experience
To initiate
To be free.

Meanwhile,
I'm a coward.
I yearn.
I yearn.

Coward!

DE-FENCED

You may not feel, yet,
Wild
Nor
Free
But do you see
The horse, ungaited blue, quietly
De-fenced?
Distant mountains, sky and trees,
Unfocused still,
Await your touch to make them
What you will.

Damn Damn Damn

Damn, damn, damn!
And so,
Moments of passion pass
Like my life,
Contained
Controlled
Experienced
Intensely within
But held tightly
Curled inward
Bound
Or trying to bind
The upward surging,
The rising Spirit
Determined to overflow
The locked floodgates
Of life's dam.
Don't push the river?
But why dam it?
Both dammed rivers
And dammed emotions
Produce electricity.

AND SO I WAIT

And so I wait,
Looking,
While waiting,
Searching,
Like Rudy Wiebe,
For a human,
A free spirit,
With whom to dance,
To celebrate life
Now.

I, Alone, Am Responsible For Me

I, alone,
Am responsible
For me.

Alone,
I search in vain
For some one,
Any one,
To be
Responsible for me.

Trapped inside the lonely circle
Of myself,
I gallop wildly,
Searching for an out
From me,

Knowing
Inwardly
That it is not
To be, knowing
That I can bear
The burden
Of my Self.

Awareness

Is
An ever-expaaaaaaaaaaaaaaaanding horizon   . . .

BLIND

He doesn't see
You;
He doesn't see
Me;
He doesn't see.

Eyes,
Shadowed by
Ego needs
Are
Sightless,
Not capable of looking
Outward
Or
Inward.

Missed Cues

A glance
Turned away,
A smile
Unrewarded,
An outreached hand
Ignored.

Lighted lamps
Snuffed out,
Fleeting chances
Passed over.

All, everyday signals,
Gone
Forever,
Evaporated
In life's misty
Consciousness.

On Mountain Climbing

What force lies within
That drives me to
Climb to the summit
To view from
It's pinnacle
The valley below?

To finish the climb
Is not reason enough
But to explore
The rocks and crannies
Along the path
Keeps alive the desire,
The expectancy
Of discovery, of hope.

Is hope
Enough
Or
Will I turn back,
Exhausted?
* * *

Some inner voice
Says,
"No, you will not turn back.
You may go
Slower;
At times you may sit
And rest awhile,
Even fall
Slipping backwards towards
Former ways of being
But,
There's no way back, for you,
Not now,
Not ever."

I Sit By The River, Alone

I sit by the river
Alone
And watch the gulls
In groups
Placidly floating
In the quiet backwater of the
Faster-flowing mainstream.

Cars, trucks, busses,
Crisscross the highways
Noisily,
All going somewhere;
The destination only needed to justify
The busyness.

I sit alone, still,
The fall sun warm
On my back;
The quiet breeze
Fluttering the page,
White, translucent,
On which I record
The crisscrossing pathways
Of my journey.

The further I go into myself
I go alone;
Life's traffic and noise
Closed out.
Even the language
Is unknown to me.

I struggle to communicate
My awarenesses,
Not to control
But to keep the gates
Swinging open,
On two-way hinges,
Between our two, very separate, worlds.

I struggle for words, concepts
To express my thoughts, feelings
But my inept attempts to communicate
Too often
Become a challenge
Against which

The gates snap shut and
My communication becomes
Pleas, demands.

Unheard, rejected,
I go from aliveness, vitality,
An ability to struggle with
The overarching issues of life
To deadness.

Vitality fades, yet,
I know,
Somewhere deep inside,
That I will try again
To unlock the gate and
Hope again to
Commune
With you.

Separate Worlds

We don't work
Because we can't
We live in two separate worlds,
I in Spirit
You in Matter.

Really one,
But when unacknowledged,
Spirit hides
Failing to enliven Matter
And
We remain

Earthbound.

My Teetertotter

Surprised by joy?
Surprised by sadness?
Either/or
Equally surprising
50/50 chance
Life's teetertotter,
Life's see/saw.
Does joy have a price
To pay?
Does sadness?

Is the hawker
And purchaser
Of either
Joy
Or
Sadness
One and the same,

Me?

Unsorted Emotions

Unsorted emotions
Fettered freedom

The task:
To sort the emotion
To unfetter the freedom.

GIVE ME

Give me what you can offer
Without
Regret or hesitation,
And
I will do the same.

I, only, am responsible for Me
And for that which I choose
To give
Or share.

Freedom, for me,
Is in the choice of giving
Or withholding.

And what I give
Is mine, alone,
And of your gifts
That which I accept
I make my own.

A lonely choice
The only way to share
What is
Without regrets.

The only vow
We make
Each to the other
Is one of
Total honesty,
An inward
Search of
Motivations.

You cannot be
Responsible
For me
Nor can you ease the pain
Of my wanting
That which you cannot give.

For in withholding
You are taking
My responsibility
From me
And shouldering
More
Than is rightly yours.

Delicate balance,
This freedom
And
Responsibility.

ALONE

Alone,
A condition of the journey.
Born alone,
Travel alone,
Die alone,
What then?

What I see, hear, and feel
Conditioned by others,
Perhaps,
But I alone
Weave them together in my way,
Creating my path,
Step by step
Lesson by lesson.

Inevitably,
My way is different from your way,
My friend.
How could it be otherwise?

And so, my understanding
Of the journey
Departs a way
And that's okay.

The Dream, The Reality, The Question

The Dream
I could feel my eyes sparkle
With sexual mischief,
Thinking of the illustrated Kama Sutra
Lying on the sale table
In the downtown
Bookshop.
Our fifth business!

"Let's look!" I suggested,
Thinking that
Fifth businesses
Seldom
Get taken care of
In the routine of
Business one and
Business two
And three
And four.

A conspiratorial sharing
Of sensual pictures
Is what I'd impishly
Suggested,

Sexy conspiracy
In a book loft,
Up a winding, spiraling
Staircase.

A fun thing
To do,
A quick, defiant gesture
Delaying, for a moment,
Routines
and
Responsibilities.

The Reality
A twisted arm,
A reluctant partner.
No conspiratorial glances
No sexy giggles
No joy or silliness.

"Buy it; take it home,
If you must," you said,
"Who wants to look here?
Not me!"

Not me?
True enough,
Not me either!
Spontaneous sharing?
Indeed,
A leaden moment.

"Let's go home," you say,
"Get gas;
Pick up shoes."
You complain about the price
Of soles and heels,
"Next week the price
Is going up some more."

The price is going up
Again
And so it has
Already.

The Question
What is the price of me?
How much am I
Willing
To pay
Over and over,
Again
For leaden moments, instead of joy
What price?
What price?

ODE TO EASTER: BOUNDARIES

Boundaries,
If lightly held,
Are easily
Transcended,
Cracking gently with
An easy touch.

But boundaries,
Thick and overgrown,
Resist the gentle probe
And grow thicker still,
Smothering the
Emerging Self
Within.

When the Self,
Waiting to be born,
Is strong
It can smash a thickened shell,
Pent up energy
Powerful life force
A tool,
Tiny pick
Or a sledgehammer,
Depending on the need.

A life and death struggle
Takes place
At each new birth;
The death rate never computed
A mortician never called.

ODE TO EASTER: GROWTH AND SHELL CRACKING

The sun's rays surge
Through the window of myself,
Warm ocean swells of energy.

My Inner Self responds,
A spirit stretch,
Symbolic arms extended in greeting
To the sun.

Long fingers stretch
And gently touch
The fragile, translucent
Shell encasing me,
Knowing that
These fingers soon will
Less gently push.
My shell must grow—or break.

And I remember
This day is Easter,
Symbolic of new birth,
Life,
Growth.

My life has been an Easter egg,
Colored,
Pretty,
Lifeless.

And I think of other eggs,
Natural, protective ovals,
Downy chicks
Emerging,
Tiny, moist creatures,

Life grown too large
For their surroundings;
Protection became confinement
And life burst forth,
Broken shells strewn
About the nest.

ODE TO EASTER: WHEEEEE!

Why should I
Be
Surprised by
Joy
When I am
Its
Creator?

I, my total Self,
Not just
My will
But by my Spirit,
Released
By me
To beeeeeee,

Wheeeeeeeeeeee!

I AM

I am.
There is no beginning;
There is no end.
I am a circle,
Endless,
Perfect.

I am creation. I am life.
I am a breath of wind
Ruffling the leaves,
Whispering softly,
I am.

I am a baby's cry
Soft at first,
Then insistent
Demanding milk,
Essence of life,
In order to be.
I am.

I am fire,
Burning,
Consuming--
Reducing all
To basic elements

In order to be
Re-created.
I am.

I am lightening
Flashing across the
Dark sky;
Energy, raw
Unleashed,
Recharging
Electrifying.
I am desire
Urgent,
Insistent
Surging to re-create.
I am.

I am the ocean,
Salty, endless swells
In the ebb and flow
Of the tide.
I am.

I am a tiny stream
Leaping over pebbles,
Rocks and boulders
Rushing to the sea.
I am clear sparking water,
Cold,

Moist,
Refreshing,
Life-sustaining.
I am.

I am a blade of grass,
Green in spring;
I am a sheaf of wheat,
Heavy with grain,
A robin's egg.
I am the sun,
Hot,
Radiating,
Energy.
I am.

I am.
There is no beginning;
There is no end ...
I am a circle,
Endless,
Perfect.
I am nothing;
I am all.
I am.

A Pile Of Papers

A pile of papers,
Interviews
A job
Time,
Held in my hands

Burst into flame
Curl
And turn to
Ashes,
Crumbling
Through my trembling fingers.

Ashes of moments,
Past
Moments
Of life,
My life.

I hold in my hands
Moments
And they turn to ashes
Quick burst of
Energy,
A flame,
Gone.

I hold in my hands
Moments
Can they be of my choosing?
Can I be a
Co-Creator of my
Life?

Or
Do I hold only
That
Which is handed
To me?

To My Inner Self

Because of you
I sing my song.
I sing my song
Of joy and gladness
Because of you
I am made whole again.

Because of you
I have been
United
Re-united with
My Self.

I sing my song
With eyes wide
Open
Because of you
I sing my song
With you and gladness,
My song.

My song is filled
With tender moments;
My song is filled
With ecstasy.

You are my song
My song of
Gladness.
You are my song;
My Spirit's
Full and
Free.

I gave myself
In
Love
Completely
And the river did
Answer with
It's song.
A song of joy,
Pure exultation.
A song,
My song.

A Lilac Bush

A lilac bush
Purple and white
Wet with
Gentle rain
Grows near the
Walkway,
Sending
Fragrant invitations
By wind messengers.

I Come To Visit My Sunflowers

I come to visit my sunflowers
To say hello
To me.

A quiet time
To meditate
To let ideas float
While stooping low
To pull a weed
Or break a
Clump of earth,
Watching it crumble
And fall
Through my caressing fingers.

I planted the seeds
In sunlight, morning's glow,
But there
My labour's ended,
And
I can do no more.

Each seed will germinate
Or not
Depending on its core,
Small kernel of energy
Within
That'll burst its bounds
Once sun and rain
Have again performed
Their re-creating
Miracle.

Sunflowers,
I will come
Again,
Come
To lie here
On earth's moist bosom
Inhaling her warm aromas
Intoxicating scents.
I will lie here,
Arms stretched to the sun
Recharging my Spirit,
My Self
With life-giving rays.
Here, sunflowers, I am me!

I Dream, I Dream

I sit on the highest mound
In our meadow
and
Dream dreams.

Of people free to be themselves
To know
And to respond
Not only to what
Life brings but
To create
A life
That springs from living
Attuned to inner senses,

Experiencing
Fleeting moments
Now—or
Never.

SELF-DELUSION

My capacity
For self-delusion
Is endless.

Illusion
Upon
Illusion
Discovered
Only to find another
Underneath.

Endless varieties,
Tiring
Exhausting
Work
This.

SEARCHLIGHT

Eyes
Turn inward
Flashing search lights
Sweeping corners
Dark crannies
Fearless
Piercing.

Don Juan Says...

Don Juan says
Twilight is the crack
Between the worlds,
The door to the
Unknown

And

Twilight brings
To me
Bittersweet nostalgia…
Yearnings
For unknown
Worlds
Within,
Without.

ADVICE TO MYSELF

Gather thy
Rosebuds
While they be
And don't bemoan
The morrow…
(careful those thorns!).

Gather,
Gather,
Gather.

For when they're dried
And winter's here,
Their faint aroma
You will savour

Until, in another distant
spring,
You will gather again
And remember.

I Need A Path

Locked in mortal battle
With myself
On different planes
In different fields
One battle
Oft repeated
In essence the same
Again
And
Again.

The issues?
Strength or weakness?
Duty or desire?
Freedom or responsibility?
Intellect or emotions?
Sanity or insanity?

Where's the path?
Where are the guidelines?
Where,
Oh,
Where?

Sadness, Flood The Earth With Your Tears

Ebb and flow,
My sadness comes;
My sadness goes,
It is real.

Traces of sadness.
Traces?
Tides of sadness.
Deep, swirling oceans
Of sadness
And just my thin shell
Of muscle and skin
To contain the ocean.

Why should it be contained?
Let it swell
And howl and cry
And flood the earth
With its tears.

Harsh Words

Your torrent of words
Cascade over
My body,
Icy shower
Shriveling
My Spirit,
Condensing
The rising vapor
Into spiritual
Teardrops.
Once again,
Spiritual genocide.

Harsh words,
Like harsh winters,
Icy blasts,
Are soul-shrivelers.
I wrap the layers
Of myself
Around my Spirit
To keep me warm.
My spark,
Glowing ember of life
Can only be snuffed out
By me.

Spiritual suicide's unthinkable.

I wait for a gentle breeze
Of summer's love
To fan
Into flame
The glowing embers,
Smoldering within.
Someday…

Meanwhile,
I not so passively
Wait
As before.

I Offered You My Soul

I opened up myself,
My shell,
And offered you
My Soul.

You changed the subject
And talked
About a book for
Recording messages
So we would not only
Get them
But they'd be catalogued
By day, as well.

Automatic history.

You did not hear
My message;
It's not in your
Message book.

Nor will it ever be.

THE LAMP WAS LIT

The day was tense;
No, we were tense, tired
Tempers flared
Frowns
Irritability.

Are we hiding in work
That we have nothing
To say to us about us?

We talk about the project
As long as I don't ask questions;
We talk about the trees,
Eaten by mold,
But we don't talk
About a marriage
That needs.

Tonight a lamp was lit,
A small flame
In the darkness
To say
Let's try
Let's try
Let's …

Your reading light, turned on,
Drowned the flame
And you were silent,
Hidden behind the pages of your article.

Cry   Cry   Cry

I'm tired of crying;
I'm tired of trying,

So go on reading,
My dear,
Go on
Go on   Go on.

Because
I, too, have gone
Just now.

JOY

Joy is a song
Waiting to be sung;
A song out there
Somewhere
Or so I've been told.

It gives me
Pleasure and
It gives me consolation
To think of a song
Floating,
Slowly dancing, waiting
For me
Somewhere.

But joy is not out there
But in here,
Inside of me,
Floating,
Slowly dancing, waiting
For me
To allow
Me
To be sung.

I Don't Want To Be Heard

I don't want to be heard,
Nor understood,
Nor wanted
By you
Anymore.
No more.
No more.

It's easier to go in anger
Or in hurt
Or need.
It's easier to justify my going
If you are somehow responsible
But you are not.

For you are you
And I am me
No longer is there a troublesome we.

And I have gone,
Been gone
For a long, long time.

Fat Bird

Fat bird
Impudent and sassy
Swinging, almost free,
Above the bed post.

I am watching
You,
You well-fed, chubby pigeon
Impish grin and
Insolent swagger.

I am watching,
Seeing you,
Your inner freedom
Not quite matched
With outer.

Teasing bird.
He also is watching
You;
Him,
The inner guardian
Against free spirits
And free birds.

He is watching,
Watching and grumping,
"Go back, little bird,
Go back to the two-tiered,
Well-teared cage
With door ajar
Back to the cage
And the thin, thin bars.
Shoo, little bird,
Shoo.
Go in, go in."

I am watching, little bird,
Watching as you allow
Yourself
To be shooed
Into the wire cage
With the thin, thin bars
Bottom wiggling
In sexy swaggers.

I am watching, little bird,
Watching your hip-swiveling
Dance
Upon the wire shelf,
A dance performed as if
For yourself, alone,

Knowing that He,
Your former guardian,
Is a guard no longer.

He has no power
To force you back, back
To the cage with the
Thin, thin bars.

You know;
He knows
But still pretends
To guard
Or
Be guarded.

Whichever.

Inside/Out

I am being turned
Inside out
Upside down
Something is pulling
From the heart
Outward,
An invisible drawstring
Reversing my be-ing
And
Revealing my
Self,
My Soul,
For the discerning eye
To see.

Emotions,
Raw,
Exposed.

ANOTHER LAND

I ventured
Almost by accident,
Tiptoeing carefully
Into a hushed solitude.

I ventured
Into another world
A separate reality
Tiptoeing carefully,
Senses alive.

Hushed solitude,
Quiet bower
A moment in time
Yet timeless.

Alone,
Together, with you.
There by decision
There by fortunate accident.
Totally there,
Senses engaged.

Alert,
Hushed
Waiting.
Serendipity?
Not quite.
Time stood still
For us
For me
For you
Waiting…in
Magical moments
For us
To
Know.

My Psychic Pool

Turning on the hot water tap,
I muse as windows and mirror
Fog over with steam.
I press my brief, but expanding,
Satchel of memories
To my center,
To me,
As I step deliberately,
Knowingly,
Into my private body of water,
My ocean.

You have profoundly
Disturbed my psychic pool
Waves lashing the shores,
Pounding my rationality,
Eroding my banks,
Tossing fence posts
And locked gates
Aside
Like match sticks.

You who heed not red lights,
And stop on green.

I Long

I long
To look at your face
In the night
To hold it in my hands
To trace the lines
To swim in your rivers
To walk in your valleys,
I long.

Equal Partners

A message of hope
This painting is,
Knowing
That rocks do survive
The ocean's storms,
Enduring
Wintery blasts,
Tumbling
Resistant
Eternal
Losing particles that
Crumble to sand
Warm under bare feet.

The ocean waits
Calm
Knowing
That the rocks will
Endure
Tumbled smooth
By its storms
Equal partners,
The rocks and the ocean
And
The storm.

My Choice

I chose life over death;
Praying to feel alive,
Not knowing the pain
Involved in feeling.

It's more comfortable to be
Numb completely,
Dead,
Than to be alive,
In pain.

Still,
I choose
To
Live my life
Alive.

All Of Me

"Mr. Davies, Sir,"
I asked,
Heart thundering unexpectedly,
"You recommend in your book,
Fifth Business,
That one should shake hands
With one's own devil,
Elder brother of God,
And I agree.

I've come that far,
Don't you see,
That much I've done,
That much,
But
What then?
Mr. Robertson Davies,
What then?"

Mr. Robertson Davies
Peered over
Gold-rimmed glasses,
Scholarly, rotund,
He stroked his
White and flowing beard.

"What then?" again I asked.
He mused,
"Well, you see,
Shaking hands
Is enough,
An acknowledgement
That one's own devil
Exists,
But
One doesn't have to make him
A bed partner,
Don't you see?"

Expectations fled
Disappointment flooded,
"Is that all
You have
To tell me, Robertson Davies?
That much
I know already!
I've come that far,
But, Mr. Davies,
Mr. Davies …"

Mr. Robertson Davies turned
Aside,
Claimed by another,
"Goodbye, Mr. Davies,"

I softly said.
And I sat,
Again alone,
Re-Knowing,
Ruefully
(Why is it so hard to learn?)
That any
Oh so tentative
Truths
Are not to be found
In any other.

The process sounds so easy;
No mention's made of
Sleepless nights,
The hours of painful sorting,
Hurtful truths
And agonizing sobs.
The process's never easy
But one thing I am certain of
That when the sorting's done
By all of me
Then my devil
And my God
And me—
We all agree.

I Am Lonely Here Without You

I am lonely
Here
Without
You
Grey,
Life suspended,
Waiting
Yet
For what I know
To be.

The time is
Right, almost,
For me to be
With you.
I cannot wait
Forever,
Stifling
My inner cries.

Black, Apache tears
Glisten
Translucent
In the sun.

Old Woman

Old, old woman,
Who are you?
Face that's traveled
The centuries,
Face lined with living
With loving
With sorrow
With tears.

Old, old woman,
Who are you?

Who are you?
Eyes that sparkle
With laughter
And knowing
Eyes, deep, deep brown
Eyes that see
What others cannot.

Old, old woman
Are you here?
Will you answer
My call
Will you be near?
I need you now.

Teach me
What I need
To know.

OH STONE

Oh stone,
Grey, smooth,
Long
Seemingly selected
Idly
From the bank of the river
By my lover
And me.

My fingers caress
The length of your
Soft/hard smooth skin
And I know
You,
Nature's stone,
Pulsating
With cosmic vibrations
Of the centuries.

How many years
Have you lain
Here, waiting?

Oh stone,
Filled with
Old Man River's spring swellings
And the
Icy groans of his winters,
His sunny calm and serenity too.

Stone, tumbled by conflicting
Currents
Pounded, broken, smoothed
Tossed on the river bank
To lie, until
We came,
United in spirit
He, me and you.

From what boulder were
You born?
From what mountain?
Were you split by
Earthquake, ice or
Lightning's fire?

Oh stone,
Ejected, rough and jagged,
Were we to be your destiny?
Were you fashioned
By the universe
As a blessing on
Our union?

Are you a part of us or
Were we fashioned
From your being?

Oh stone,
Oh sacred stone.
Hello.

Against The Current

United spiritually,
In beautiful harmony,
We sat by the river,
Old Man River,
The sun warm on our backs
That day.

Against the rushing,
Swollen
River current
A beaver swam,
Slowly
Resting momentarily,
Feet clutching the overhanging bushes,
Before swimming again,
Against the rushing,
Swollen
Current.

Yukon Grandmother Speaks

My daughter, you must continue
The journey you started.
It will be hard.
There will be rocks,
Boulders,
And floods.

Floods of tears and yet
There will be
Moments of joy and peace,
Moments that must not
Be clutched or grasped
But experienced fully
For what they are.

You, my child,
Are here to cut a path
Through the wilderness
To burn stumps
And clear timber,
To set fires,
Burning the old
So that new life can flourish.

Don't be afraid.

On Being Called A Prick

She talked of her loneliness
I talked of mine
Two souls meeting and sharing, for a time,
Separate yearnings
And separate knowings,
Though guarded somewhat.

She offered me her
Astrological knowledge;
I did not ask.
I cuddled the soft body
Of her baby
And played with her toddler.

We chatted of many things;
Not wanting me to go,
She offered me dinner,
Soup from a can,
And salad,
With apologies, though none were needed.
Canned soup? A sign of friendship, or so I thought.
I washed the dishes; she dried.
My bracelet, lying forgotten on the counter,
Was returned later

When she came to me. We drank coffee
While babies played on my
Living room floor.
Invited again into her private self, I ventured,
Unguarded and unaware
That she would not only think, but call me a prick
For entering without logic and reason
As my companions.

A prick?
Maybe I was.
Surely, I did prick something
Within her Inner Self, unwittingly
Or
Should I have stayed
On guard,
Refusing to enter,
Though asked.

Deliver Me

Deliver me from the
Clutches of those
Who
Love
Me.

Those whose very
Death
I inspire
And
Those who desire
My death
In the name of love.

Bile rises,
Intent on engulfing
My soul.

Deliver me.

My Self Is Not New To Me

My Self is not new to me;
Being quiet in my center
Is familiar.
Yet
I have stumbled here by accident
Today;
I had no conscious thoughts or methods to get me
From there to here.

I am learning slowly
To travel the pathway from the light of consciousness
To the dark realms of the unconscious
And back again,
Bearing tiny jewels of Knowing,
Enlightening the day and lessening the darkness.

I am attracted to and yet I fear
This inner journey to Knowing,
Aware that if I Know,
Truly Know,
Then I must act.

I Searched For A Teacher

I searched for a teacher, a Guru
Who would lead me to me
Yet all I have to know
Lies buried
Deep within,
Waiting
For me to insert the key
To unlock the door
To vast knowing
Deep within.

Embrace Your Death, My Love

Embrace your death, my love
Draw her close
Feel her breath upon your cheek
Luxuriate in her
Intoxicating scents
And die
That you may live.

Messengers Of Love

Two beautiful blue
Rods with
Hearts for wings
Hovered over
My lemonade glass.

Are they dragonflies
Or
Messengers of love,
I wondered?

And I entered
The stillness
Of my Soul.

Timeless Corridors Of Time

The clock ticks
In the silence.
Tick tick tick tick tick
Tick tick tick tick tick
Endless ticking, ticking.

But there is
No time
No clock
Tick, tick, ticking

No clock no time.

Time has ceased,
Plunging me into
A timeless,
Spaceless
Void.

It's dark here.

Down the dark
Corridors
Of time and timelessness
An anguished cry

Echoes and
Re-echoes.

Hear, my cries
Rend the darkness.
Cries of my soul's agony
Fill
The timeless
Spaceless
Void.

There's no one
Here.
There's no one
To hear.
No one.

So cry,
My beloved Soul,
Cry
In the spaceless
Timeless
Void.

Cry silently.
Cry loudly.
Who is here?
Who will hear?

Oh! You Did Me A Favour

Oh! You did me a favour;
You left before
I grew
Disillusioned
Of love without courage.

Courage is born
In the face of fear,
You know.

There were shadows in
Our love;
Trees without leaves,
Warm barrenness,
Oh.

Presence At The Esso Station

Your presence
Surrounds me,
Bringing unexpected
Tears and pain
As I sit
Eating
Brown toast and marmalade,
Remembering.

Across the café
A man sits,
His chin resting
On his hand,
Eyes glistening,
Listening
To the woman,
Across.

And I remember.

My body remembers
You;
My head remembers
The problems;

My heart remembers
    The joy
    And
    The pain.

My soul remembers
    Thee.

I ache; I ache.
Go away.
Leave me with
Remembering,
Barren of the pain.

Go away.
Your presence
    Is too
    Thick.

Quick Change

I can slip on my hair jacket
At a moment's notice,
Ready, instantly
To be
A martyr.

Oh, for a noble cause!

Strange

Can I not as
Easily
Become a clown,
A jester,
A buffoon or
Dancer?

FRAMES WITHIN FRAMES

Oh mountain,
Snow covered, lonely, white
You stand framed within the frame
Of my window,
Mirroring for a moment
Me to myself.

Many frames you have,
The mind's eye, mine,
A kitchen window
And
Nature's own,
Clouds,
Lake
And tree-covered hills,
And many more
Beyond my vision.

As I muse,
An autumn leaf
Falls down
And
I remember
That song of yesteryear,
Nat King Cole

And Emily,
College roommate of my youth,
Crooned their song of autumn
While yet in spring
Unknowing
Of the days to pass.

Now I stand in an
Autumn of my Autumn
A leaf falls down.
Nat King Cole, long
Has lain in
Mounded ground;
Grey-haired Emily,
Her songs,
Ripened now,
Have fallen
Like autumn leaves
Returning to the soil.

And what of me?
My song
I would sing it yet
Beyond the Autumn
Sing it yet
As snow falls down
Sing it yet
As spring's warmth
Returns the leaves
Sing it yet.

And yet …

NO WORDS

Words cannot open
That secret place,
Cannot reveal
The mysteries
Locked within.

Reason cannot
Enter;
Thoughts
Left behind.

That dwelling place
Of Spirit
Belongs to itself
Alone.

It is not mind;
It is not matter;
It is Spirit.

And Spirit cannot be seen,
Nor touched.

So why am I
Trying to capture
You
In words,
Oh, Spirit of Mine?

Leaving Words And Worlds

My heart
In slow, rhythmic beats
Penetrates
Deep
Within the darkness
Of my understanding.

Deep woods
Mind-less-ly entered, leaving
Familiar worlds
Far behind.
Leaving words
Far behind.

Thick silence.

Enigma

An enigma
You are
Will you always
Be so?

When you go inside
Yourself,
You know
I cannot follow;
You lock the door.

Are you running
From
The Old Woman?
She will surely
Follow you,
Go where I cannot
and
Dog your path.

I am tired,
And I am afraid
That I've done it again
Found someone
Who locks
Doors against
His Self,
The Old Woman
And
Me.

ZEUS

Thundering through caverns
Zeus throws his lightning bolts
Electrifying,
Cracking open
Imprisoned oceans
Of Knowing within.

Wise Beyond Measure

You are wise beyond measure
Yet you have measured
Oh so carefully.
What's so wise in measurement?

Be it better to be
The fool?

WE KNOW NOTHING UNTIL

Two old psychics
Together
Discuss
Interesting theories,
Material garnered from
Sources unknown or surmised.

Funny, how
Much we assume
And how little
We know
For sure.

Yet forever
We live
Unknowingly
Until
The heart
Is enlightened,
Informed and
Infused
By love and
By light
From the Soul.

No-Thing-Ness

My musings
Have evaporated
Into
No-thing-ness.

No thoughts
Invade the sanctity of
The electric
Stillness.

HIGH FREQUENCY SILENCE

The cat wants in.
I'm restless and cold.
You sit in your chair,
Head back,
Feet up.
Waiting,
The both of us
For
someone
To speak.

And then,
I hear
The silence
Whistle past,
The silence,
A laser,
Burning through skin, and bone and cell
Coring
My core,
My essence.

Vibrating,
Liberating,
Raw.

High frequency silence,
Mission completed,
Retreats
From whence it came
And
I am freed.

False Pride

Out of a sense
Of being
A nobody,
He
Fashions
His pride.

Touch Of Spirit

Your touch
So light upon my skin
Enfolded me
Warm and soft
and
The sun
Engulfed my soul.

A Cat In The Sun

A cat
In the sun
I am

Gathering

Warm rays
Inward.

I Cut Off The Wellspring

I cut off the wellspring
Of my love
With fears of dryness and of drought

Realizing
Not yet fully
That my fountain
Flows from within to without.

You Say There Is No Anger

You say there is no anger
Then why the pounding heart
And why the churning stomach,
Twisting to hide
The tangled web inside?

You say there is no fear
Then why the dilated eye,
The pounding head,
The tightened jaw
Stifling
The scream within?

Why, oh why?
Why the studied calm
And why the measured voice,
Why the rational, intellectual argument,

Why?

I Don't Like

I don't like
The silent treatment.
I don't like
Silent martyrs.
I don't like
Self-righteous saints.
I don't like
Shut doors.
I don't like
Rejection.
I don't like
Being labeled.
I don't like
Being alone and lonely.
I like less
Being together and lonely.
I don't like
Feeling my heart being squeezed.
I don't like
Relationships that aren't!
You, my erstwhile partner,
Are not.
You meet emotion with intellect and
Intellect with emotion.

Tangled webs,
Tangled, tangled.
Enough,
Enough.

Let emotion deal with emotion;
Intellect with intellect.

Together, they will help you find
Your lost and lonely Self.

LEGALITY AND LOVE

Legality is needed
When love breaks down.
Being in tune
With universal law
Had been mistakenly
Understood by you.

Universal law,
If you will
Call it that,
Is a law of Love.

You cannot legislate Love;
It is not,
And will not,
Be subjected
To legality.

Legality is of the ego's domain.
Legality is born from fear;
Fear of losing some thing,
One's belongings,
One's boundaries,
One's rights,
One's control.

The Soul cannot be regulated
By law and legalities;
It can only regulate itself, by itself,
By Love.

Drip, Drip, Drip

Drip
Drip
Drip

Glucose, saline water and death
Slowly penetrate
Your body
Fighting each other,
A no-win battle for life.

Death,
The final reality
Or
What *Life* lies beyond
A seemingly
No-win battle?

Outside/Inside

The outside
world
And the inside
Are
One
And
The same.

HE WALKS IN FEAR

He walks in
Fear
Throughout the land
Not knowing
He is one
With it,
Formed from its clay.

Taking a handful,
He'd fashioned himself,
His body,
Sturdy,
Solid,
Beautiful,

Yet, he remains un-enlightened,
Heavy,
Fearful
In his un-knowing.

I Have Walked Oh So Far

I have walked
Oh, so far,
Endless miles
Searching for you,
Oh, Thou, my Love.

And I am tired.

Bathe my feet;
My burning soul
Needs comforting
And sleep.

Lie with me,
Oh, my Love,
Enfold me
In your mantle
And I will
Sleep.

BEING IN A STATE OF LOVE

Like a beautiful piece of art,
The act of making love
Arises from an inner state,
Expressed outward.

I do not need the outer expression
In order
For love to be real.
It is wonderful
To paint, sculpt, dance or make love,
But not essential
To my
Be-ing.

I do not need an object
to complete my sentence.

I am

Love

Embodied.

I Look Up

I look up
Expecting to see you
Standing on the porch,
Looking out to Sea
But you're not there
Not there,
Not here
Except in my dreams of you.

And, yet, you're here
Somewhere,
Deep inside my Self,
How or when or where you got there,
I do not know.
Lover, son or brother
You are there, were there.

And now, you've disturbed
My psyche,
Yet again.
You leave it shattered
When you go
And when you come
A spark
Lights anew within my Soul.

SPIRIT JOURNEY

Now I begin
My journey
Above the clouds
Drinking in
The essence of me,
The universe,
And
Thee.

Now I begin
Now I end
Now I am
Eternal.

Mindless I come
Mindless I go
Mindless
Eternal mind
In control.

In dreams
I wander the universe
Unknowing
But knowing
All.

In dreams
I fly
Over obstacles
That are only there
In my mind,
Dark shadows that
Fade away
When illumined by my
Mind
Eternal.

WHERE ARE MY BOUNDARIES -- WHERE ARE YOURS?

Where are my boundaries
Have I none?

Am I me,
You,
Us,
All?

Is it my heart,
Your heart,
Our heart,
The heart of all?

Is your heart
My heart
Our heart
Or the heart of all?

If you darken your heart,
Are you darkening
Yours,
Mine,
Ours,
The heart of all?

Is darkening darkening
Or
The process of en-lighten-ing?

I need to know!

Tired

I am sitting here
Day after day;
Am I waiting to be rescued,
From what or whom
I do not know
And

Who or what is this
Inner Voice
I wait so patiently
To hear?

Speak, oh Voice,
Speak words of wisdom
Speak words of rhyme
Speak words of prophecy
Speak
Words or no words.

But no words come
From any Inner Voice;
A score of words come
From me…
Re-hashing, Re-shaping, Re-working
Me.

Oh, I am tired.
I no longer want to look at me;
I've looked enough.
I want to look at
You through me
Or
Me through you.

I'm tired of going it
Alone.

Speak To Me

Great Spirit, speak to me,
Tell me what I ought to know.
What is this upsurge of urgency,
This racing heart,
These unexpected tears?

My feet,
Are planted solidly
On the ground;
I've done my work, and more.

What yet? What yet is there to do?
Speak, and I will hear, oh One.
Great One, Shining One,
I have always sought after you,
Followed your light when the night was dark,
Oh One! Great One! Shining One!
Don't elude me now.
I have come.
I am tired.
I want to know what Thou hast in store
For me,
For others
And for You.

****

My daughter, you have truly spoken.
You have followed me well.
You have done your work and more, 'tis true
And now, there's more, ah, more.
Many will need a guide,
A loving hand, a word, a touch,
A signpost true,
That's what you are.
'Tis yours, 'tis yours, this path;
You've forged the way;
You've walked
Unerringly,
Despite your lack of knowing
Where your feet did trod.

GIVE UP ALL

You must be willing
To give up
Everything
To follow me—
Houses and lands
All.

All fears and phobias
Compulsions
Have to's
And
Want to's
And
Guarantees.

And mind
Must yield
To Mind Eternal,
Mine,
Not mine,
Trusting in
Not-knowing,
Knowing.

You must come to me,
Hands outstretched,
Empty,
Waiting
To be filled.
And I will fill
You.

UPSIDE DOWN

Upside down
Our world lies
180 degrees wrong;
Upside down
Not right side up,
And who will
Right the wrong?

It lies in lies
And in illusions,
The illusion that true
Is false
And false is true--
That what we are
Will never do.

And so,
To right the wrong
We strive life long
To become
What we are not
And thus confound
Our Selves.

In His Body...

In his body
He carries the seeds
Of his sickness,
Nourished
And
Cherished
By thoughts of darkness
And of drought.

And,
In his body
He carries the seeds
Of his wholeness
Nourished
And
Cherished
By thoughts of happiness
And of love.

Two worlds, within
One fighting
One waiting,

Patiently, lovingly
For the time
When he will wake,
Knowing that the choice is his.
Knowing,
Really knowing,
Who he is.

I And Thou Are Here Already

Oh God,
My creator,
And my creation,
Me.
I no more
Cry out for Thee,
Unknowing
That Thou art in me
And I in Thee.

Oh foolish heart,
Oh eyes so blind
Oh ears so deaf that
I could not feel, nor see,
Nor hear
Thy call
Not from without
But from
Within.

I ask no pardon
No belated blessing
Save from myself
To me,
For Thou were
And always are
In harmony and love
With me.

Laugh, oh Thou
My heart
And dance,
Oh Thou my feet,
Sing
Oh Thou my mouth
Re-joy-see,
Laugh
And dance and sing
In praise of Thee—and
Me.

No House Needed

As I venture further and further
Inside
This makeshift house
I've built to protect
Me from the cold,
I gradually discover
That I need
No house,
No protection.

I stand,
Not exposed,
As I expected,
But transformed,
Open to renewing and recreating
My Self.

POINT NO POINT

Point no point
Point no point
Lovers come and lovers go
Point no point
Summer comes and summer goes
Point no point
Flowers bloom and flowers die
Point no point
Light house beams a flashing light
Pointing still.

FIERCE LITTLE WOMAN

Battling death
Fighting to keep
Her man, trying to
Hold death at the door,
A one-woman struggle
To hold back the tide
Abandoning God
In her struggle
To delay the
Inevitable.

The Raven Plays

Lone,
Against the sky,
The raven plays,
Surfing the crest of
Unseen waves.

As do I.

I am not as trusting,
Yet, as he,
Nor skilled,
Falling heavily
From sky to
To earth,
Again and again.
Hurt, broken.

There I rest,
Until
Re-energized by
Mother Earth and Spirit,
I rise to
Soar again on
Unseen winds
And waves.

DON'T SPEAK

Don't speak,
My Soul
Don't say the words
That I don't want to hear.

Hearing would crack
My silent solidity
And I would know
What I would not.

No, don't speak.

Pixie Dust

She had said her goodbyes
She wanted to go,
Curious about what new delights
Awaited her in
The great beyond.

Pixie she was;
Pixie she is,
Scattering her magic dust
As she flies
Free
From her body
Held prisoner
By the unrelenting hand
Of death.

We stand
Hearts peering intently
Trying to perceive
Her flight
Dimly knowing that magic
Dusts lies
Sprinkled on our hearts.

COMMUNION

Inside the very heart of me
Is me,
My Self,
Hidden
Deep
Where inner/outer
Oceans merge
And flow.

From Self, from Spirit or from Soul,
I stream towards
My Creator.

Becoming one,
I float
On the tide,
Storms subside
Peaceful,
Safe
In the very heart of me.

Don't Talk

Shhhh
Shhhh
Don't talk, you say.
He's gone?
He died?
He killed himself?
Fie!
Shame!
Don't talk.

You don't ask why.
You don't ask how.
You don't try
To understand
His pain nor
His reasons
For taking that gun
And killing himself.

I need to talk
I need to cry
I need to fill the spaces
Where he was
With words
With reasons
For his death.

I need to fill the spaces, those
Empty, empty spaces
With love.
With understanding
With peace.

When you don't want to hear
What I need to say
You rob yourself
And me.

You rob yourself of knowing
Who he was…
And why he was,
And what he was
And why he took
That gun and killed himself.

Could it be that he was heroic?
Could it be that he was brave?
Could it be that he wanted to live, to laugh,
To love, to feel alive?

He did not want the
Cancer
To devour his dignity,
His voice,
His very breath,
His freedom.
To choose his fate.

And so he made a choice,
(isn't that the ultimate freedom?)
He chose to end his pain
Curled in a blanket,
An Indian blanket given in love.
And, overlooking the sea,
He left,
Quickly, surely, quietly.
He left.
And I grieve my loss and yours.

So, allow me my tears, my words
Allow me my grief
So that I, and you, can fill those empty spaces
With love
With understanding
With peace.

I Lie Awake

I lie awake;
I listen to the night
Filtered through my body
And my brain.

Coyotes howl
The rain comes down,
"Who?" cries the owl,
Calling my Soul.

"Come!"

"Come fly with me."

GOD CALLED AND I ANSWERED, UNKNOWINGLY

God called me
To be me
And
I have put all kinds of other names
On that calling.

Why don't I say that God called?
That I heard my name?
Why don't I say,
Like Samuel of old,
"Here am I, Lord,
Here am I."

I don't have trouble with saying
That God called my father …
Out of a little town
Into a littler one.

Did my Dad ever wonder
Why he left everything behind
To follow that call?
I wonder.

So this morning,
This lovely, sunlit morning,
I am saying,
God called,
Is calling,
Has been calling
For a long, long time.

Here I am, Dear God,
Here I am…
Here I have always been
Unknowing,
Yet knowing,
A woman of God,
A woman with God.

Me.

A Secret Love

Oh my Love,
My secret Love,
Dreams of You
Comfort me
Through the days
And the long, long nights
Of sorrow, longing
And grief.

I yearn
I yearn,
Total, unfulfilled yearning.
I long for connection,
For touch.
My Lover has departed for distant shores;
He is here no more.

And yet ... and yet ...

No one knows that
At times in the long, dark night,
My secret Love,
Conjured up,
Brings comfort that sustains me
Through the lonely night.

No one knows,
Not him,
Not them,
Just me.

WOMAN OF WISDOM, COME NOW!

Old Woman,
Woman of Wisdom,
Come now!
I need you.
I long to be held
In your embrace.

I would have you
Shower me with your grace
So I again can plumb the depths
Of this, my ocean.

Deep, deep down
Where there is
No-thing-ness.

No-thing
but me and you
And Them.

Us,
One.

Mountains Rise Up Pink

The mountains
Rise up pink;
Their sheer
Peaks,
Reflecting rays
From the fading sun,
Illumine
My uplifted vision.

Shadows,
Cast by
Un-illumined
Granite,
Outline,
By reflection,
The mountain's strength,
And mine.

The Poems

Am I A Myth?   1

Waiting For The Word   2

Dying And Heaven   3

Guardians   4

Where Is The Me?   5

With You, I Need No Defenses

I Walk In The Cemetery

On Growing

Labour Pains

Walls Within Walls

Surprise Attack

Mirror Reflection

I Reason Against The Reason

Free Spirits Are Timid Creatures

Hurt, Tears, Anger

Who Knows?

I Know More About You Now

Ego Monster

Opt Out

My Self Is Heavy

Words Are Barriers

Duty Walks With Heavy Tread

Dance Of The Rings

Pilgrim At Tinker Creek
Ode To A Listener …
Desire Is A Vapour
Locked Box
Who Are You?
Let Me Go!
Do I Have Time To Wait?
De-Fenced
Damn Damn Damn
And So I Wait
I, Alone, Am Responsible For Me
Awareness
Blind
Missed Cues
On Mountain Climbing
I Sit By The River, Alone
Separate Worlds
My Teeter-totter
Unsorted Emotions
Give Me
Alone
The Dream, The Reality, The Question
Ode To Easter: Boundaries
Ode To Easter: Growth And Shell Cracking
Ode To Easter: Wheeeee!

I Am
A Pile Of Papers
To My Inner Self
A Lilac Bush
I Come To Visit My Sunflowers
I Dream, I Dream
Self-Delusion
Searchlight
Don Juan Says …
Advice To Myself
I Need A Path
Sadness, Flood The Earth With Your Tears
Birth And Death
Harsh Words
I Offered You My Soul
The Lamp Was Lit
Joy
I Don't Want To Be Heard
Fat Bird
Inside/Out
Another Land
My Psychic Pool
I Long
Equal Partners
My Choice

All Of Me
I Am Lonely Here Without You
Old Woman
Oh Stone
Against The Current
Yukon Grandmother Speaks
On Being Called A Prick
Deliver Me
My Self Is Not New To Me
I Searched For A Teacher
Embrace Your Death, My Love
Messengers Of Love
Timeless Corridors Of Time
Oh! You Did Me A Favour
Presence At The Esso Station
Quick Change
Frames Within Frames
No Words
Leaving Words And Worlds
Enigma
Zeus
Wise Beyond Measure
We Know Nothing Until
No-Thing-Ness
High Frequency Silence

False Pride
Touch Of Spirit
A Cat In The Sun
I Cut Off The Wellspring
You Say There Is No Anger
I Don't Like
Legality And Love
Drip, Drip, Drip
Outside/Inside
He Walks In Fear
I Have Walked Oh So Far
Being In A State Of Love
I Look Up
Spirit Journey
Where Are My Boundaries—Where Are Yours?
Tired
Speak To Me
Give Up All
Upside Down
In His Body
I And Thou Are Here Already
No House Needed
Point No Point
Fierce Little Woman
The Raven Plays

www.ingramcontent.com/pod-product-compliance
Lightning Source LLC
Chambersburg PA
CBHW051054160426
43193CB00010B/1179